PRO ART
FLUTE and PICCOLO
METHOD

Book 1

A first year course
for individual or class instruction

by
Donald J. Pease

PRO ART
PUBLICATIONS

PRO BK 520

Rudiments of Music

Before we begin the study of a musical instrument a knowledge of the rudiments of music is necessary.

A Musical Sound is called a TONE. Every tone has three properties: 1. Length, 2. Pitch and 3. Power.

Musical tones are indicated by symbols called NOTES. The time value of each note is determined by their color (black or white) and by their form (by stems and flags, etc., attached to the note). The following notes are in most common use:

Whole note ○ ,   Half notes ♩ or ♭ ,   Quarter notes ♩ or ♭ ,

Eighth notes ♪ or ♭ or ♫ ,   Sixteenth notes ♪ or ♭ or ♫ .

The STAFF upon which music is written consists of five horizontal lines and four equal spaces.

LEGER lines are added lines placed either above or below the regular staff to increase its range.

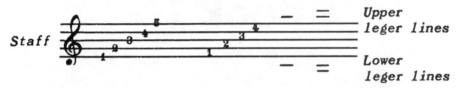

The staff is divided by vertical lines called BARS. The space between the bars is called a MEASURE.

The CLEF sign: Treble or G Clef placed at the beginning of the staff gives a definite pitch to the lines and spaces of the staff. It establishs the pitch of G on the second line of the staff.

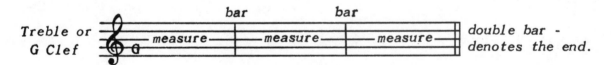

To name the lines and spaces, the first seven letters of the alphabet are used: A B C D E F G.

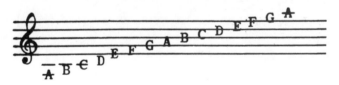

NOTES are placed on the staff to represent musical tones. Notes determine the length of the tone. RESTS are placed on the staff to indicate silence. They are classified as follows:

Name	Note Symbol	Rest Symbol	Value in Common ($\frac{4}{4}$) Time.
WHOLE	○	▬	4 counts or beats
HALF	♩	▬	2 counts or beats

Name	Note Symbol	Rest Symbol	Value in Common ($\frac{4}{4}$) Time
QUARTER	♩	𝄽	1 count or beat
EIGHTH	♪ or ♫	♎	1/2 count or beat
SIXTEENTH	♬ or ♬	♎	1/4 count or beat

The value of each measure is indicated by the TIME Signature (numbers) which follow the clef sign. The UPPER figure, tells the number of beats found in each measure. The LOWER figure, indicates the kind of a note that receives one beat or count.

SIGNS MOST COMMONLY USED

' Breath mark. Indicates where a breath may be taken.

Hold or Pause. 𝄐   or 𝄐 A sign placed over or under a note or rest signifies that it is to be prolonged more than its ordinary value.

Repeat Signs. 𝄆 ⋯ 𝄇   The dots placed before a double bar indicate a re-petition of the preceding part or section.

D. C. al Fine means to return to the beginning of a piece and repeat it to the sign 'Fine' or 𝄐 Fine means the end.

D. S. means to return to the point where you see the Sign (𝄋) and then proceed to the Fine. D. S. means from the sign.

Staccato. A dot placed above or under a note ♩ or 𝅗𝅥 signifies the note is to be played de-tached or short.

A Dot (.), placed AFTER a note or rest prolongs its value by one-half its original value. Example: 𝅗𝅥 plus . = 𝅗𝅥 + ♩ = 3 beats.

Legato sign is a curved line  connecting two or more notes. It means that these notes are to be played smoothly, in a connected manner.

The TIE is a curved line connecting two or more notes of the same pitch; notes connected by a tie are played as one note. Example: ♩͜♩ = 𝅗𝅥

Sforzato (>): notes so marked are played with special stress and emphasis. Example: >𝅗𝅥 or ♩>

Tenuto is a dash mark over or under a note ‾𝅗𝅥 or ♩̱ denoting it should be well sustained (played broadly).

Fingering Chart for the Flute and Piccolo
(Boehm System with Closed G♯ Key)

The fingering for each note is given when the note is introduced for the first time in the lessons, and should be LEARNED at that time. Use the chart only for necessary reference. In case more than one fingering is given, use the first one unless otherwise specified in the lesson.

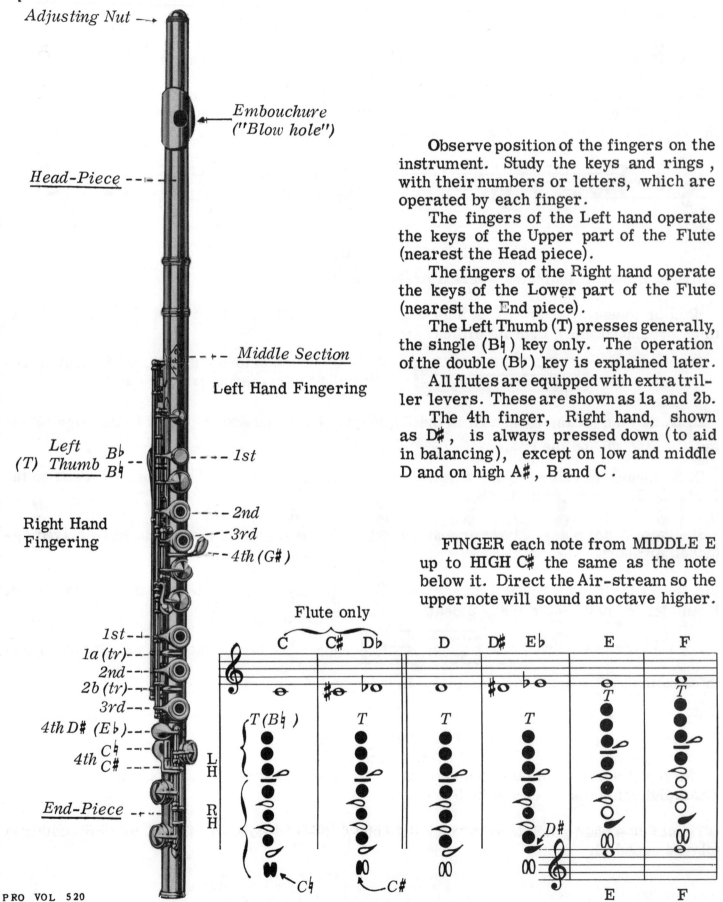

Adjusting Nut →

Embouchure ("Blow hole")

Head-Piece

Middle Section

Left Hand Fingering

(T) Left Thumb B♭ B♮

Right Hand Fingering

1st

2nd
3rd
4th (G♯)

1st
1a (tr)
2nd
2b (tr)
3rd
4th D♯ (E♭)
4th C♮ C♯

End-Piece

Observe position of the fingers on the instrument. Study the keys and rings, with their numbers or letters, which are operated by each finger.

The fingers of the Left hand operate the keys of the Upper part of the Flute (nearest the Head piece).

The fingers of the Right hand operate the keys of the Lower part of the Flute (nearest the End piece).

The Left Thumb (T) presses generally, the single (B♮) key only. The operation of the double (B♭) key is explained later.

All flutes are equipped with extra triller levers. These are shown as 1a and 2b.

The 4th finger, Right hand, shown as D♯, is always pressed down (to aid in balancing), except on low and middle D and on high A♯, B and C.

FINGER each note from MIDDLE E up to HIGH C♯ the same as the note below it. Direct the Air-stream so the upper note will sound an octave higher.

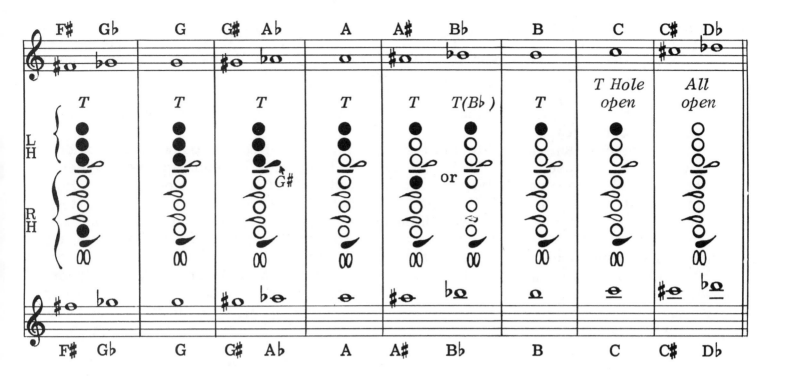

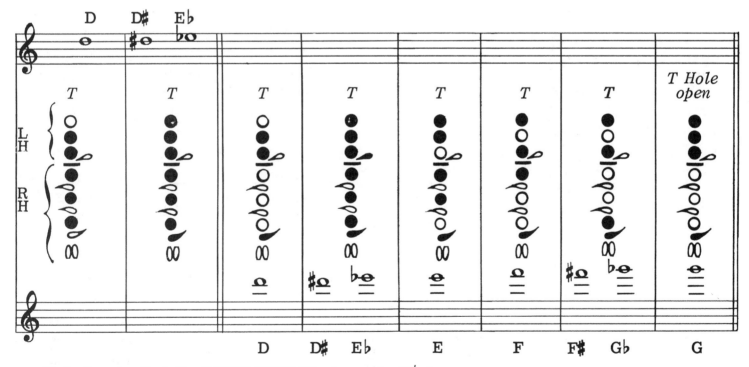

T Indicates that the LEFT THUMB closes in B♮ key.

● Indicates the hole is to be covered.

○ Indicates the hole is to be left open.

Keys marked with various (——→) figures or letters are to be pressed down as indicated.

Instructions to the Student

CARE AND ASSEMBLY OF THE INSTRUMENT

In order that your instrument will sound its best, it is of utmost importance to keep everything pertaining to the instrument in perfect playing condition.

1. Put your instrument together carefully, according to the instructions and with the guidance of your teacher.

2. The mechanism (keys, etc.) of the Flute is very delicate and should be handled very carefully. In assembling the Flute, remove the protective end caps from the ends of the main joint (long part) and the head joint (which includes the "blow hole"). Hold the main joint near the upper end in the left hand and fit the foot joint (shortest part) to its proper place. Then hold the main joint in the same place by the right hand and with the left hand place the head joint in the proper position. Avoid grasping the Flute in a manner that might bend or damage the springs or keys.

3. After using the instrument, wipe it dry both inside and out. Special cleaners (swabs) are made for this purpose. Wooden instruments should be oiled (inside) at least once a month. Consult with your teacher. All joint corks should be greased frequently with joint grease. Occasional oiling of the mechanism (key springs) is suggested. Don't use too much oil - just a drop.

4. When not in use, always keep your instrument in the case.

CORRECT POSITION, HOLDING AND FINGERING OF THE INSTRUMENT

1. Proper posture whether sitting or standing is very important. Always stand or sit Erect, with the head up. The arms, hands and fingers should be completely relaxed, without stiffness. Breathe normally. Support the breathing by using the abdominal muscles.

2. The Left hand covers the keys on the upper (nearest the "blow hole") part of the instrument. The first three fingers cover the holes (keys) on the upper part of the main joint. The Left thumb covers the B♮ or T (Thumb hole) on the back of the instrument.

3. The Right hand covers the keys on the lower (nearest the foot joint) part of the instrument. The first three fingers cover the holes (keys) on the lower portion of the main joint. The Right thumb is placed on the back, opposite the fingers and aids in balancing the instrument. The Right fourth (little) finger covers the D♯ key, which should be used at all times unless otherwise indicated.

4. The hands and fingers should be relaxed. Play using the finger tips, keeping the fingers close to the keys at all times. Keep the fingers curved (slightly arched) forward.

TONE PRODUCTION (EMBOUCHURE)

At first, practice using the head joint only. Place the edge of the "blow hole" against the center of the lower lip on a parallel line with the red part of the lip. A little experimenting will help you to locate the right place. The lips should be formed so as to produce an opening which is small, and shaped like this: ▸◂▸◂ The lip corners are held tightly together. The size of the opening between the lips will depend on the results desired.

In producing a tone, after assuming the correct lip position, the air should be directed in a steady stream against the outer edge of the "blow hole". The quality of the tone may be regulated by rolling the head joint in or out until the right position is found. The tone on the Flute is started by snapping the tongue. The tip of the tongue is placed near the upper front teeth. The tone is started by quickly withdrawing the tongue and pronouncing the syllable "Tu" (too). Be sure no air escapes out of the corners of the lips. Do not breathe through the instrument but through the side of the mouth.

PICTURES ILLUSTRATING CORRECT POSTURE, HOLDING AND FINGER POSITIONS

Correct
Playing
Position.

Embouchure
Lip and "Blow
hole" position

Hand and Finger
Positions –
Top View

Introducing the First Three Notes

The TONE, which sounds at a certain pitch are called NOTES. The notes are written on or between five lines which is named the STAFF.

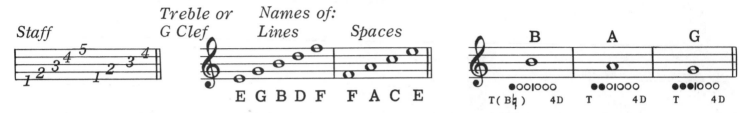

The Flute may be held easily, if properly balanced by side of first finger of the Left hand, the thumb of the Right hand, and supported by the fourth (little) finger of the Right hand resting on the D♯ key. The R.H. fourth finger should always be used as a support to all notes <u>except</u> a few shown in the Fingering Chart.

Left Hand

Right Hand

T indicates that the Left Thumb closes the B♮ key.

The Whole Note (o) and Whole Rest (━) receive 4 beats each.

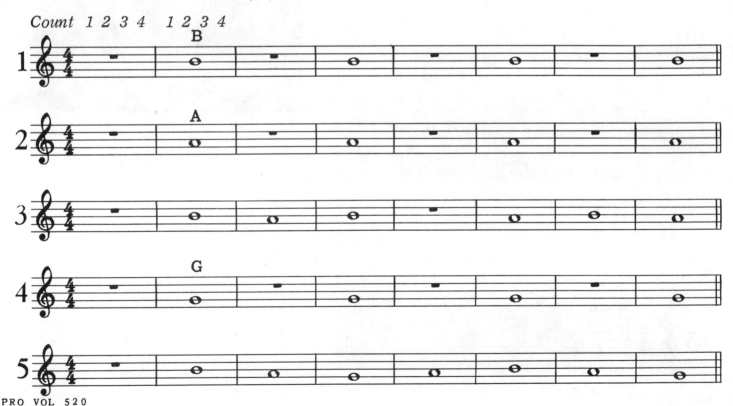

Whole Notes and Rests

In C or $\frac{4}{4}$ measure, each whole note or whole rest receives four beats.

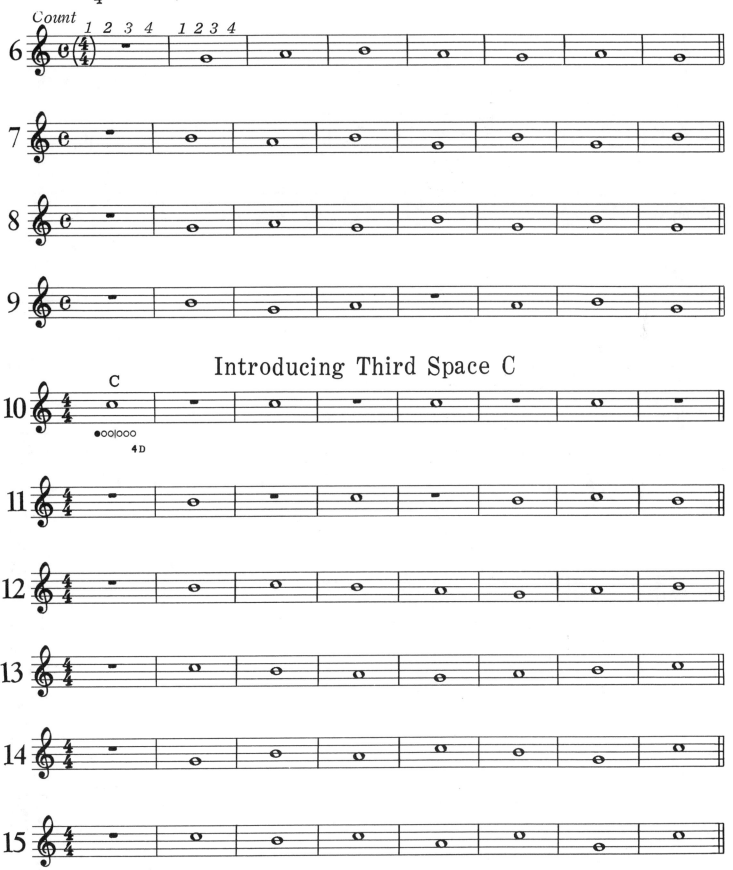

Introducing Third Space C

The Half Note and Rest

HALF NOTES
= 2 beats each

HALF RESTS
= 2 beats each

Steady counting

Our First Melody

D. J. Pease

*, breath

Skipping Around

Our First Song

D. J. Pease

Avoid taking a breath after each note. Play several notes to one breath as indicated by the (,) breathing sign.

The Quarter Note and Rest

In C or $\frac{4}{4}$ measure, each quarter note (♩) or quarter rest (𝄽) receive one beat.

Merrily, We Roll Along

Melody

D. J. Pease

The Quarter Rest (𝄽)

Introducing the Lower Tones

(Played with the Fingers of the Right Hand)

Introducing Low F

Watch those Skips. (Intervals)

Practice steady counting.
Play slowly , at first.

* Introducing Low E

To the teacher: Should the student, at this point encounter difficulty in producing the tones below F, it is suggested that you skip to page 16 and defer this material until a later time.

Introducing the Tie – Dotted Half Note

The Tie (⌢⌣) connecting two or more notes of the same pitch, indicates that they are to be played as one continuous tone.

Example: ♩♩ = 𝅗𝅥 (2 beats)   ♩♩♩ = 𝅗𝅥. (3 beats)

Introducing Low D

Down We Go

Introducing the Sharp

A Sharp (♯) raises the note to which it applies by one-half tone.

A Happy Tune

Allegretto (moderately quick)   D. J. P.

Play soft and lightly

It's Fun to Play Together

Chorale
(Duet - Two Parts)

The Chimes

On the March

An Old Hymn
Tune:"Hamburg"

Evening Song
Schumann, Adpt.

Three - Quarter Time

3 ⟵— Three counts in each measure, Count 1-2-3.
4 ⟵— A Quarter note (♩) receives one beat.

The Dotted Half Note.   A dot placed after a note increases the value of the note by one half.

Example: ♩ plus • = ♩.
2 plus 1 = 3 beats.

Our First Waltz

German Folk

Waltz in G

To and Fro

D. J. Pease

Changing to the Middle Register

The Flute (Piccolo) is an octave instrument. The lower two octaves are fingered alike with the exception of third line D. (See Ex.1.below). By using the same fingering as for the lower notes and simply changing the blow hole angle and using more force in blowing, the higher notes are produced. Strive for an even, smooth, tone quality. Lip control is important.

"Forward" March
D. J. Pease

Lightly Row
Folk Tune

Old MacDonald's Farm
Folk arr.

Introducing the Slur or Legato

The Slur (⌣⌢) indicates that all notes within it should be played in one breath. Only the first note should be tongued.

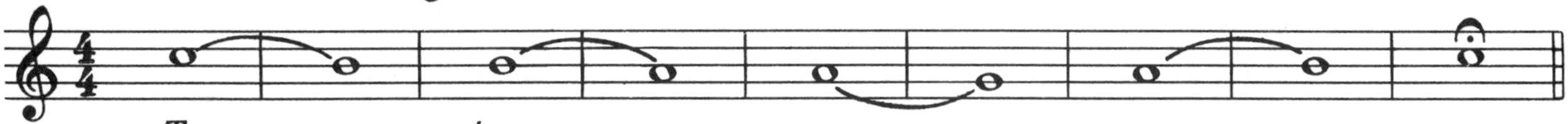

Tu - - - - - - - etc.

Tu - - - - etc.

Softly Glide

D. J. Pease

How Can I Leave Thee

Folk Song

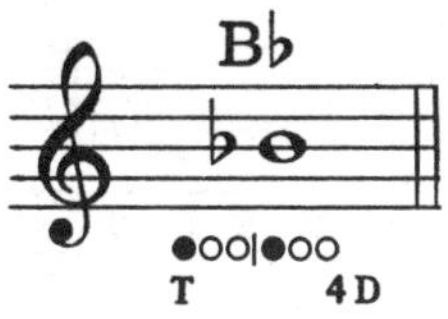

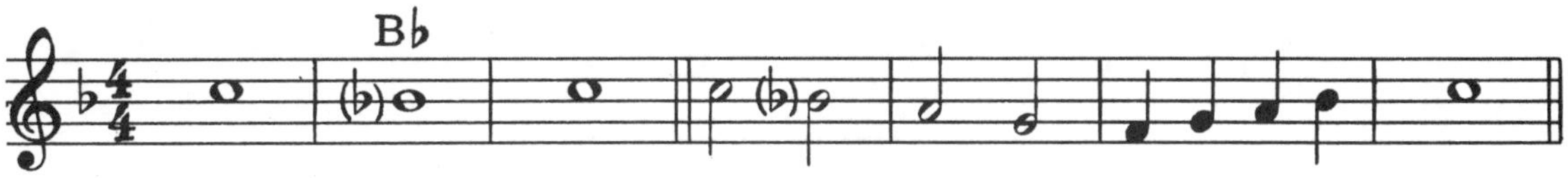

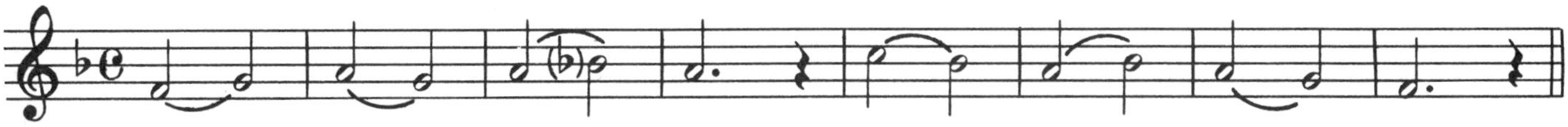

Twinkle, Twinkle Little Star

Key of F Major

In the key of F Major, all the B's are flatted (lowered one-half step) by the flat (♭) in the key signature.

Scale of F Major

Practice three ways

Thirds

Folk Song

French

Blow the Man Down

Sea Chanty

Melody

Ambrosio

Key of G Major
(One sharp-F♯)

In the Key of G Major, all the F's are sharped (raised one half-step) by the Sharp (♯) in the key signature.

When playing in the Key of G major, think F♯.

Scale of G Major

Practice three ways

Duke Street — *Hatton*

Sun of My Soul — *Monk*

Speed Our Republic — *Keller*

Eighth Notes and Rests

The eighth note (♪) is equal to half the value of a quarter note. Two eighth notes equal one quarter note.

Introducing $\frac{2}{4}$ Time ← 2 Counts in a measure.

← A quarter note (♩) equals one beat.

Theme from "Surprise Symphony"
Haydn

Jingle Bells

Long, Long Ago
Bayly

D.S. al 𝄐

Folk Melody

There's Music in the Air

Blue Bells of Scotland

Yankee Doodle

Scale Study

Dotted Quarter and Eighth Notes

A dot after a note is equal to one-half the value of the note it follows.

Example: ♩ + ♩ = ♩. (3 counts)   ♩ + ♪ = ♩. (1 1/2 counts)

America

Country Gardens

English Air

Fine

D.C. al 𝄐

College Song

Studies in the Key of C Major

(Two octaves)

*Note: Low register tones are best produced by blowing slowly and very gently into the "blow hole".

Southern Roses

Strauss

Folk Song

Auld Lang Syne

Scotch Air

Duet- O, Sanctissima

Sicilian Air

Melodies for Christmas Time
Deck the Halls

Traditional

We Three Kings

Hopkins

O Come, All Ye Faithful
(Adeste Fidelis)

Duet-Silent Night

Gruber

Key of B♭ Major

(Two flats - B♭ and E♭)

Keep the 1st finger (left hand) UP on D and E♭.

My Faith Looks Up to Thee

Lowell Mason

America

March - Onward Christian Soldiers

Sullivan

Introducing Alla Breve (Cut - time)

In $\mathbb{C}$ or $\frac{2}{2}$ Time; o = 2 beats, $\downarrow$ = 1 beat, $\downarrow$ = 1/2 beat.

Comparison with $\frac{2}{4}$ Time(meter)

Count   1   2 | 1   2 | 1   &   2   & | | 1   2   & |

Good King Wenceslas
Trad. Carol

Count   1   2   &   1   2   &

America, the Beautiful
Ward

March time

Melodies in Cut-Time (¢)

1

Pleyel's Hymn

2

Billy Boy

3

Red River Valley

4

Hand Me Down My Walking Cane

5

When the Saints Go Marching In

6

Variations on a Theme

Mozart

Andante from "Orpheus"

Gluck

rit.

Ciribiribin

Pestalozza

Key of D Major
(Two sharps - F# and C#)

Andantino

Lemare

The First Noel

Trad.Carol

Gavotte

Gossec

Amaryllis

Ghys

Staccato Study

Reuben and Rachel

Krambambuli

Student Song

Wearin' of the Green

Irish Folk

Key of F Major - Higher Octave

Blue Bells of Scotland

Melody from "Orpheus"

Offenbach

Vilia from "Merry Widow"

F. Lehar

Key of F Major
(Continued)

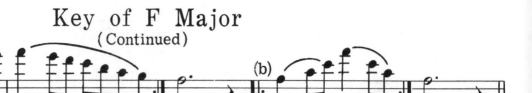

1

All Through the Night
Welsh Air

2

I Dream of Jeanie
S. Foster

3

Scale Study

4

Apply these different articulations to the above study.

(a) (b) (c) (d)

Six-Eight Time

Practice the following studies beating <u>six</u> to a measure, slightly accenting counts 1 and 4. (<u>1</u> 2 3 <u>4</u> 5 6)

Then repeat the studies beating <u>two</u> to a measure, so that the first beat falls on the count of 1 and the second on the count of 4. Slow <u>1</u> 2 3 <u>4</u> 5 6 Fast <u>1</u> - - <u>2</u> - -

Sweet and Low

Barnby

Drink to Me Only

Old English

Six-Eight Time
(Two Beats in a Measure)

Row, Row, Row Your Boat
Round

Three Blind Mice
Round

Vive L'Amour
College Song

For He's a Jolly Good Fellow
American

March from "Faust"

Chas Gounod

On Wings of Song

Mendelssohn

rit. e dim.

When Johnny Comes Marching Home

Lambert

Trio to "Our Director" March

Bigelow

More Six-Eight Rhythms

Sonatina

Andantino (Slowly)   *Mozart*

The Lorelei

Silcher

Believe Me, If All those Endearing Young Charms

Moore

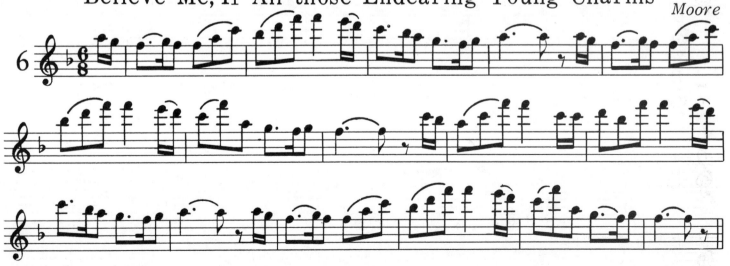

Key of A Major

(Three sharps - F#, C#, and G#)

First practice slowly in **C** time, then in **¢**. Apply different articulations shown on page 20.

For the Beauty of the Earth

Kocher

Cielito Lindo (Duet)

Mexican

Chromatic Etude

Hohmann

Key of E♭ Major
(Three flats - B♭, E♭, and A♭)

Up We Go

The Minstrel Boy

Irish Air

D.C. al 𝄐

Blue Danube Waltz

Johann Strauss

More Melodies in E♭ Major
Merry Widow Waltz

F. Lehar

Lullaby

Johannes Brahms

Come Dance and Sing

English Folk

Chromatics

same fingering

same fingering

Sixteenth Notes

A Sixteenth note (♬) is equal to half the value of an Eighth note.

♬ = ¼ beat   ♬ = ♪ ½ beat   ♬♬ = ♩ 1 beat

Rhythmic Variations using Sixteenth Notes

Study

Peasants Polka

Listen to the Mocking Bird

Old MacDonald's Farm

My Maryland

German Air

Battle Hymn of the Republic

Wm. Steffe

Theme from Military Symphony

Haydn

Largo from "New World Symphony"

Largo (very slow, broad)

Antonin Dvorak

Last Rose of Summer

Andante

Flotow

My Heart at Thy Sweet Voice

Andantino

Saint-Saëns

Studies in G Major

Chord Study

Slurring Etude

Limbering Up Exercise

Londonderry Air

Old Irish Air

Duet-The Ash Grove

Welsh Folk

Chromatics

Chromatic means moving up or down by half steps. A chromatic scale is one that ascends or descends entirely by half steps. Enharmonic Tones are those notes which sound the same although written on a different degree of the staff. Ex. D♯ and E♭. Be sure to use the proper fingering both ascending and descending the scales.

D Chromatic Scale

G Chromatic Scale

Melodie in F

A. Rubinstein

Star Spangled Banner

Smith–Key

Minuett

Beethoven